Handbook of Faculties for Priests Serving the Mission Church

AF472095

Handbook of Faculties for Priests Serving the Mission Church

Father William T. Liebert, SVD, JCL

Copyright © 2010 by Father William T. Liebert, SVD, JCL.

Library of Congress Control Number:		2010917828
ISBN:	Hardcover	978-1-4568-2488-4
	Softcover	978-1-4568-2487-7
	Ebook	978-1-4568-2489-1

All rights reserved. No part of this book may be reproduced or transmitted in any form or by any means, electronic or mechanical, including photocopying, recording, or by any information storage and retrieval system, without permission in writing from the copyright owner.

Imprimi Potest
July 17, 2009
Mark E. Weber, SVD,
Chicago Province, Society of the Divine Word.

This book was printed in the United States of America.

To order additional copies of this book, contact:
Xlibris Corporation
1-888-795-4274
www.Xlibris.com
Orders@Xlibris.com
89186

Contents

Acknowledgment 11

Chapter One: The Meaning of Mission Church 13

Chapter Two: Baptism Juridical Incorporation into the People of God 18

- The Minister for Baptism 18
- The Catechumenate and Those Previously Married 20
- Baptism of Children 21
- Summary: 21
- Terminology 23
- Matter and Form of Baptism 24
- The Matter 25
- The Baptism Conferred in Non-Catholic Churches 26
- Conditional Baptism 26

Chapter Three: The Sacrament of Confirmation 28

- The Character of Confirmation 29
- The Matter and Form 29
- Capability of Receiving Confirmation 30
- Requirements for Confirmation 31
- The Minister for Confirmation 32
- Sponsor 34
- Receiving a Baptized Person into Full Communion of the Catholic Church 34

Chapter Four: The Sacrament of the Eucharist.................35
- Validity of the Minister 35
- Eucharistic Ministers 36
- Preaching at Mass...36
- The Homily 36
- Rights to the Eucharist 37
- Reception of Holy Communion By a Baptized Non-Catholic..........38
- Prohibition of Communion to Manifest Sinners 39
- State of Grace..40
- Holy Communion to Children 40
- Eucharistic Fast..41
- Communion Twice a Day...42
- Consecration of the Bread and Wine..............................42
- Priests Recovering from Alcoholism..............................43
- Tridentine Mass 44
- Time of Celebrating Mass..44
- Reservation of the Eucharist....................................44

Chapter Five: The Sacrament of Reconciliation................46
- The Nature of the Sacrament 46
- Individual Reconciliation.......................................47
- Obligations for General Reconciliation 47
- The Minister of Reconciliation..................................49
- Granting the Faculties..50
- Absolution in Danger of Death 51
- Revocation of Faculties 51
- Ecclesia Supplet..52
- The Seal of Confession 53

– Censures, Penalties, and Absolution 54
– Remission of the Censure 56
– In Danger of Death 58

Chapter Six: The Sacrament of Holy Orders 59

Chapter Seven: The Sacrament of Matrimony 61
– Faculty to Witness a Marriage 62
– Dispensation from the Form of Marriage 63
– Common-Law Marriages 63
– Impediments to Marriage 64
– Convalidation Because of an Impediment 68
– Convalidation of Defective Consent 68
– Convalidation of Defective Form 68
– Premarriage Instructions 69
– Dissolution of the Bond 69
– The Interpellations 71
– The Petrine Privilege 72
– Polygamous Marriages 73
– The Internal Forum Solution 74

Chapter Eight: The Sacrament of the Anointing of the Sick 77
– The Matter and Form 78

Chapter Nine: Special Blessings and Circumstances 82
– The Ministers of Sacramentals 83
– Consecrations and Dedications 83
– Ministers of Blessings 84
– Exorcisms 85

– Funeral Rites for the Dead 86
– Cremation..87
– Catholics Who Are Denied Catholic Funeral Rites.....87
– Liturgies of Marriage Marriage between
a Catholic and Another Christian 87

Index...89

I dedicate this handbook to the memory of my first bishop at Papua New Guinea with whom I had the great privilege to serve the people of God, the Most Reverend Leo Arkfeld, SVD, DD, Bishop of Wewak-Madang.

Acknowledgment

I am very much indebted to the *New Commentary on the Code of Canon Law* (study edition) by Fathers Beal, Coriden, and Green and to Father John Huels, JCD, for *The Pastoral Companion*, third edition, Franciscan Press. A very scholarly study of the history of the development of missions can be found in the book *Constants in Context: A Theology of Mission for Today* by Fathers Stephen B. Bevans, SVD, and Roger Schroeder, SVD, Orbis Books. Many of the examples are taken from my own mission experience of over fifty years in Papua New Guinea.

Chapter One

The Meaning of Mission Church

There was a time when the concept of "mission" and "missionary" clearly meant a locality that was inhabited by a people who were non-Christians and worshipped what was considered an idol or pagan god. When the known world expanded and countries began claiming lands in the New World and then in Asia and Africa, the Catholic church as well as Protestant churches began sending out ministers whose purpose was to convert the non-Christians into their faith. Catholics saw a rapid expansion of religious orders of men and women who left Europe and became missionaries. Both North and South America had hundreds of missionaries from the Jesuit, Franciscan, and Dominican orders. Many of these heroic people braved hostile tribes and were martyred, and many perished from malaria, blackwater fever, and typhus. As Africa and Asia became more known, new societies such as the Divine Word Missionaries were sent to China, Japan, and Papua New Guinea.

The Church in Rome had been active in keeping abreast of the affairs in the mission territories by first establishing a commission, then later a congregation entitled the Sacred Congregation of the Propagation of the Faith. This title was later again changed to the Congregation for the Evangelization of Peoples.

Priests working in the mission territories of Africa, Asia, and Oceania realized that they required certain faculties or permissions in order to propagate the faith. They were meeting certain circumstances with non-Christian people such as multiple marriages and petitions that were made to Rome for faculties to deal with such cases. As these faculties were given, canon-law books also changed and special-mission faculty books began appearing.

But the world changed more and more especially with World War II. Countries that had been colonies were clamoring for independence. Many countries that had been staffed by priests and religious had lost hundreds, even thousands, of the missionaries in the war. Movements toward lay participation in the Church sprang up especially through the writings of Pope Pius XII. Lay missionary groups were formed in Europe, America, and Australia. Lay missionaries literally poured into the mission fields. Another happening that was noticed was the competition between the Catholic church and the non-Catholic churches and even among the Protestant churches themselves.

A quotation from the book entitled *Constants in Content*, page 243 under International Context, is worthwhile stated here as it clearly points out what took place:

> For the Catholic Church in this period, there were five popes, four of whom were quite influential in their own way. The pivotal person was John XXIII, who to everyone's surprise, called the Vatican Council (1962-1965). This event set into motion major changes in the Church both ad extra and ad intra. Rather than viewing the "world" as totally opposed to God's reign, the Church began to "read the signs of the times" and to acknowledge the movement of God's Spirit outside the Catholic Church, leading to more open and positive attitudes towards other churches, religion and non Western cultures and society in general.

All this led to a change in the canon law of the Church so that a revision of the 1917 Code of Canon Law was required. Canon lawyers, theologians, and bishops became very active in the revision work. In 1983, the revised code finally appeared. The concept of *mission* and *missionary* had changed to fit the modern times. The whole Church began to see itself as *missionary* and that all the faithful in the Church were *missionary*. But despite all these theological changes, there are still many priests, brothers, sisters, and lay missionaries who lived in thatch huts, rode horses, or walked or begged from benefactors for money to pay catechists or those whose lives are in danger from anti-Christian fanatics.

Very few priests in these mission areas would have the money to buy the new canon-law commentaries. The missionary of today could be faced with human trafficking, drugs, drug laundering, corruption in the government, and so on. The code does not cover these subjects, but it does tell us about the sacrament of reconciliation. The missions still exist, and while books on what to do in this or that circumstances have gone out of print for the most part, there is still a need to have a handbook, which can be a handy reference for the missionary priest.

This handbook is not meant to be a searching of Roman documents on giving permission for this or that. Instead, we are going to go through the Code of Canon Law and apply the law and commentary in those particular places where it is considered to the priest living and working in a missionary situation.

The circumstances of life vary considerably from place to place. The missionary of today might be one who lives in a bush house in a jungle or one who lives in the inner city of London, Paris, Chicago, or Miami and is surrounded by Buddhists or

Muslims or animists. It is hoped that this handbook will aid any priest who uses it in his pastoral ministry.

I have written this book as a handy reference and sincerely hope that this will prove useful to priests everywhere in their pastoral care of the faithful.

Chapter Two

Baptism Juridical Incorporation into the People of God

101. A human person who is validly baptized is, by an act of baptism, incorporated into the people of God.

101.1. These baptized persons are generally referred to as the *faithful.*

The Minister for Baptism

102. The ordinary minister for baptism is a priest or a deacon.

102.1. However, anyone who has the proper intention to baptize and the recipient wants to be baptized can confer baptism in danger of death.

Application 1: A priest is summoned to the sickbed of a dying person. He arrives to find the person is unconscious. He can proceed with baptism since it is evident the person who summoned him wanted to be baptized.

Application 2: He finds the person dead when he arrives. Do not proceed with baptism of a corpse when it is clear the person has been dead for some time. However, it is reckoned a person still has life up to an hour after the heart has ceased beating.

103. The Catholic Church recognizes baptism of desire. This is clear in Lumen Gentium (13) of Vatican II. However, baptism of desire does not incorporate a person into the Catholic Church. Therefore, in such cases, do not enter the person in the baptismal registry.

104. Baptism of blood is considered the same as baptism of desire.

105. The term *catechumen* is to be used strictly for those not yet baptized.

105.1. Catechumens are “connected” to the Church in a special way by their desire to be incorporated into the Catholic Church.

105.2. The catechumenate proper begins from the rite into admission into the order of catechumens until sacramental initiation; hence, merely the intention to join the catechumenate is not sufficient.

105.3. Catechumens are granted two special privileges:

1. The right to a Catholic wedding, whether to a Catholic or non-Catholic
2. The right to the funeral rites of the Church (Canon 1183)

The Catechumenate and Those Previously Married

106. Persons who are invalidly married because either they or their spouse or both have been previously married may be admitted to the catechumenate. However, and this is very important, they may not be admitted to baptism until they are declared free to marry through either a declaration of invalidity of the previous marriage or a dissolution in favor of faith.

Application: Number 106 is very important for missionary priests. A declaration of invalidity of a previous marriage or a Pauline or Petrine dissolution in favor of faith will be taken up later. There have been cases where a proper investigation was not made, and then, more or less at the last moment before baptism, it was found out that the person has previously been married.

Application: Every mission diocese should produce a well-thought-of prenuptial questionnaire to avoid such problems as in 106. Some diocese even require that the questionnaire be submitted to the chancery before the wedding for review by a canon lawyer or experienced missionary priest before a *Nihil Obstat* is given for entrance into the catechumenate.

Baptism of Children

107. Children who die before baptism may be buried with a Catholic funeral if the parents had intended to have the child baptized (Canon 1183, paragraph 2).

Application: It would seem that even stillborn or even aborted fetus could be given a Catholic funeral. Although they were not baptized, the Church entrusts them to the mercy of God who wants all people to be saved. Obviously the feelings of the parents here should be respected. Never use force or arguments.

Summary:

107.1. If a child is born to both Catholics, baptize and register.

107.2. If born to one Catholic, one non-Catholic, baptize if parents agree, but be assured of a Catholic upbringing.

107.3. If born to an unwed mother, baptize; register the mother only unless Civil Law demands the father also be registered if the father is publically known, as is required in some localities.

107.4. If born to parents invalidly married, baptize and register.

107.5. If born to unknown parents but has Catholic guardians, baptize and register.

107.6. If born to both non-Catholic parents but one or both want the child baptized, generally speaking, do not baptize unless absolute assurance the child will be raised a Catholic.

Application: It happens in mission lands that a Protestant couple has a child, but they are far removed from their own church. For example, they were teachers or civil servants. They want their child baptized, and so they approach the Catholic pastor. The fundamental canonical principle is *semel catholicus, semper catholicus*—once a Catholic, always a Catholic. In such a case, the child if baptized by a Catholic priest is actually a Catholic. While we cannot make a definite decision here on all cases, it would seem best if the priest tactfully declines to baptize the child, informing the parents that according to our Catholic rules, if he does baptize the child, that the child actually be a Catholic and should be raised a Catholic.

107.7. If a child is born to non-Catholic parents but is in danger of death, baptize but do *not* register, and inform the parents so they can have the child registered as baptized in their own church.

Application: Here the missionary must use caution. The parents may be strongly opposed to the Catholic Church and be strongly against infant baptism. They might even try to sue the priest for baptizing their child. Catholic nurses, doctors, and midwives should be instructed in this. It may be better to have no record of the baptism.

108. Any person with the correct intention of doing what the Church wants can baptize using the correct matter and form.

Application: Missionaries should make it a special concern that Catholic nurses, doctors, and midwives are properly instructed to administer baptism as this may be necessary in emergencies in clinics and hospitals especially where there are no priests available.

Terminology

108.1. An *adult* is a person who has completed his eighteenth year of age at midnight on the eighteenth birthday.

109. A *minor* is a person below the above age to the age of seven years. Hence, at midnight, at the end of his seventh birthday, he is presumed to have the use of reason.

110. An *infant* is a child younger than seven years old and is presumed he does not have the use of reason (*non sui compos* or not legally competent).

111. A person who habitually lacks the use of reason is considered *non sui compos* despite his age and is treated as an infant.

Matter and Form of Baptism

112. For validity, this form must be used: N.I baptize you in the name of the Father and of the Son and of the Holy Spirit (Canon 850).

112.1. For validity, this formula expresses the three Divine Persons and their unity:

—the person being baptized
—the one baptizing
—the act of baptizing

112.2. The name should be used so it is definite who is being baptized.

112.3. It is no longer required that a saint's name be used, only that the name not be offensive to Christian sensibilities (Canon 855).

112.4. If the name is unknown, it suffices to say "you."

112.5. The word *I* must be used so that it is definite who is doing the baptizing.

112.6. Individually, the three Divine Persons must be used: Father, Son, and Holy Spirit. Altering this in any way, e.g., Father, Mother, etc., would be invalidating (Regatilio, Moral Theology, no. 38).

The Matter

113. For validity, baptism must be conferred with true water.

113.1. While the water should be blessed, this does not affect the validity of the sacrament.

113.2. In the mission fields, do *not* use the water from a coconut (coconut milk, Kulau), which looks like water but does not taste like water and is not water. Valid water can come from snow, ice or distilled. Invalid would be tears, sweat, liquid from plants, wine, beer, and the like.

113.3. Baptism is conferred by either pouring on the forehead or immersion in which the entire head is immersed in water.

The Baptism Conferred in Non-Catholic Churches

114. The validity of non-Catholic baptisms cannot always be taken for granted.

Application: Even baptisms by Anglican ministers cannot be taken for granted. Instead, the diocese should undertake a careful investigation to determine whether all or any non-Catholic baptisms were validly conferred.

Conditional Baptism

115. If after a careful investigation is made and there still remains a doubt as to whether the person was validly baptized, conditional baptisms may be conferred.

116. The formula for conditional baptism is "If you are not baptized, I baptize you in the name of the Father and of the Son and of the Holy Spirit."

117. If there is a doubt as to whether the person is alive and has not been baptized, the following form is used: "If you are

capable, I baptize you in the name of the Father and of the Son and of the Holy Spirit."

118. Before you conditionally baptize a person, it is only right that you explain to the person the reason for conditional baptism.

Chapter Three

The Sacrament of Confirmation

Whereby the baptized are helped to be strong in witness to their faith in word and deed and defend the faith.

—Canon 879

101. In relation to baptismal initiation, the sacrament of confirmation is a continuation of the Christian initiation.

101.1. Hence, adults who receive baptism should be immediately confirmed and receive the Eucharist unless there are serious reasons not to do so (Canon 852, paragraph 1).

101.2. Children seven years of age and over are considered adults; hence, this applies also to them.

101.3. A serious reason may be if the priest does not have chrism or the danger of death.

Application: The missionary priest may want to separate baptism and confirmation in adults in cases where he believes the adults may not have sufficient intellectual grasp and would require more instructions. This possibly could be considered a serious reason. It is a point that the diocese could determine a policy.

The Character of Confirmation

102. Because, theologically, the sacrament of confirmation imparts a special character sometimes referred to as an indelible mark, confirmation can be administered only once to a baptized person (Canon 845).

Application: Explaining the concept of *character* or *indelible mark* to some people may be quite difficult, but nevertheless, it is very important. It is this character or mark that sets the confirmed person apart as a special witness or something referred to as a soldier of Christ.

The Matter and Form

103. The sacrament of confirmation is administered by the minister by anointing on the forehead with chrism while using the words prescribed as the form.

103.1. The matter of the sacrament is chrism blessed by a bishop. Chrism is consecrated by a bishop on Holy Thursday or on Holy Week. He cannot delegate this authority to a priest. If the diocese is vacant, the chrism can be obtained from a neighboring diocese. A retired bishop can consecrate chrism.

103.2. The minister anoints the recipient by touching the forehead with chrism on his thumb while saying the words. He does not impose his hand over the head of the recipient while doing the anointing.

104. The words said at the anointing are "Be sealed with the gift of the Holy Spirit" (Canon 880).

There is a following prayer. *All-powerful God* does not pertain to the validity of the sacrament.

Capability of Receiving Confirmation

105. Any baptized person can receive confirmation.

105.1. Generally, the sacrament is conferred between the ages of seven and sixteen.

105.2. If the minister judges there is a serious reason, confirmation can be conferred *at any age* even below the age of seven; for example, in a remote area where the bishop can seldom reach.

105.3. In danger of death, a baptized adult or even an infant can be confirmed.

Application: Missionary priests should carry an oil stock of sacred chrism on going on missions to visit outlying villages.

Requirements for Confirmation

106. Apart from danger of death, the person should be suitably instructed and properly disposed and able to renew one's baptismal promises (Canon 889).

106.1. A person without the use of reason is presumed to be in the state of grace since they would be unable to commit a serious sin.

106.2. Such persons for example, with mental retardation can be confirmed. Dioceses should develop proper catechetical programs and not take it for granted they are completely unable to think.

106.3. It is advisable that diocesan premarriage questionnaires have a question on whether the person is confirmed or not. If not, then special instructions should be given so that, if possible, confirmation is given before the wedding.

The Minister for Confirmation

107. The ordinary minister for confirmation is a bishop.

108. A priest who has the necessary faculty to confirm by law also validly confirms.

108.1. A priest who has pastoral care may confirm a person who formally gave up his Catholic faith but who returns to practice his religion. There is a special rite for this (Canon 883, paragraph 2).

Application: This faculty by law is not given to any priest but only to a priest with pastoral care. Most missionaries, therefore, would be included. However, a priest doing only teaching would not be included and would need the faculty from the bishop.

108.2. A priest with pastoral care may confirm a person who was baptized but, through no fault of his own, was brought up as a non-Catholic as in 208.1.

Application: Both 208.1 and 208.2 are applicable in the mission lands. The person must be baptized of course, either as a Catholic or in a valid baptism as a non-Catholic.

109. A diocesan bishop, when a case of need requires it, can grant the faculty to one or even more priests to confirm (Canon 884, paragraph 3).

109.1. A case of need could be a very large diocese or the absence of a bishop for long periods. If there is a doubt about whether there is a need, grant the faculty anyway (opinion of canonist Wersterman, 85, quoted by Huels, page 69).

Application: It would seem from experience that some mission bishops are not aware of 109.

110. Any priest may confirm a baptized person in danger of death (Canon 883, paragraph 3).

Application: Missionaries are often not informed about this faculty. Therefore, it is important that missionaries have the sacred chrism with them in the mission travels.

In case of doubt whether a priest has the faculty under the law as he must be in pastoral care, except for 110, the matter should be submitted to a canon lawyer for his advice as there is the possibility that his conferral is invalid.

Sponsor

111. There should be a sponsor for the one being confirmed. If possible, the sponsor should be the same as the sponsor for baptism.

111.1. Parents are excluded from being the sponsor.

112. The confirmation should be recorded in the confirmation registry book according to the diocesan rule.

Receiving a Baptized Person into Full Communion of the Catholic Church

113. See the Rite for Receiving Baptized Persons into Full Communion of the Catholic Church.

114. In case of infants and older persons not having the use of reason, see the Rite of Bringing a Baptized Child into the Church found in the Rite of Baptism of Children.

Chapter Four

The Sacrament of the Eucharist

This is whereby the faithful, presided over by a priest possessing the power of holy orders, pray together, and have the message of salvation proclaimed to them and, together with the priest, offer the sacrifice to the Father of Jesus Christ and receive the bread and wine, the Body and Blood of our Lord as their spiritual food and drink.

Validity of the Minister

101. Only a validly ordained priest can validly confect the Eucharist by saying the words of the Eucharist and intending to consecrate it.

Application: While the above may be well-known to most Catholics, there are groups of laity led by a priest in some places who profess the lay group acting alone can confect the Eucharist.

Eucharistic Ministers

101.1. The ordinary ministers for Holy Communion are a bishop, priest, or deacon.

101.2. In case of need, a priest may appoint a lay person, male or female, as an extraordinary minister to distribute Holy Communion.

Preaching at Mass

102. Priests and deacons enjoy the faculty by Canon 764 to preach everywhere with at least the presumed permission unless a competent authority has restricted so.

Application: Missionary priests, especially on furlough and traveling, do not require the faculty to preach from the bishop where they are saying Mass unless this has been restricted.

The Homily

103. The homily is, strictly speaking, a form of preaching within the liturgy given by either a priest or deacon (Canon 767, paragraph 1).

103.1. Preaching within the liturgy by a lay person or lay religious should be termed a *reflection* or *instruction*.

There should be sufficient reasons for this, such as instructions to children.

103.2. The priest is obliged to give a homily on Sundays and holy days of obligation unless there are serious reasons for omitting it.

Application: Serious reasons could be for a missionary not knowing the language or illness. In the missions, it is common for the priest to use an interpreter. There have been problems with this in which the interpreter ends up giving the sermon of his own. Training is needed.

Rights to the Eucharist

104. Anyone who is baptized and not prohibited by law may receive the Eucharist.

104.1. A person who has not the use of reason and, therefore, cannot distinguish the Body of Christ from ordinary food or is not in the state of grace or is excommunicated cannot receive Holy Communion.

Reception of Holy Communion By a Baptized Non-Catholic

105. If there is a case of danger of death or a serious need in the judgment of the bishop, the minister of Holy Communion may administer Holy Communion to a baptized non-Catholic (Canon 843, paragraph 4).

105.1. The person must be validly baptized.

105.2. The non-Catholic must be unable to go to their own minister for communion.

105.3. The non-Catholic must spontaneously ask for Holy Communion.

105.4. They must manifest Catholic faith regarding the Eucharist.

105.5. They are properly disposed.

Application: Number 305.4 and 305.5 are open to very wide interpretations. How is the priest going to really known if the person is disposed? This has been open to a lot of discussions; for example, the Church requires that Catholics be in the state of grace, but all that is demanded of a Protestant is that he be disposed!

Prohibition of Communion to Manifest Sinners

106. Those who have been excommunicated or interdicted after an imposed or declared sentence and others who steadfastly persevere in manifest grave sin are not to be admitted to communion (Canon 915).

106.1. Persons who are divorced and remarried outside the Church (not divorced only) would be such an example.

Application: Missionaries will frequently come across Catholics who divorce according to local custom and then remarry or Catholics who take another wife or wives. You can attempt to explain this rule of the Church to them and hope they will respect it, but it does not always work for many people in such mission areas; it simply does not sink in. Simply passing over such people at the communion rail would most likely be disruptive and cause many to leave the faith altogether.

106.2. There is the case of persons in the political life or civil service or the medical profession who advocate abortion.

Application: These cases should be discussed in diocesan meetings, and a policy should be established that can be publicly announced. Somehow it is important to get such people to respect the Eucharist and not come to receive.

State of Grace

107. Canon 916 says that a priest should not celebrate or a Catholic should not receive Holy Communion if he is conscious of being in grave sin. The same canon states that there is a grave reason that a person, priest, or layman may make a perfect act of contrition with the resolve to go to confession as soon as possible.

107.1. A perfect act of contrition is true sorrow for sin based on the love of God. Contrition based on fear or hell or shame is imperfect contrition.

Holy Communion to Children

Most children will be prepared for their first Holy Communion. Therefore, the handbook will only deal with special situations.

108. In danger of death, a child may receive viaticum even if they are not properly prepared. All that is required is that they can differentiate between ordinary food and the body of Christ (Canon 913).

109. For children and persons with mental disabilities, there is no special arrangements made for such cases in the canon

law; however, these persons should not be just ignored as the degree of the mental abilities vary considerably.

Application: In almost every mission trip that a missionary priest will take, he will come across such cases. Rather than ignore them, the priest should urge that special programs be developed in the diocese to aid the parents and teachers to come to the assistance of such persons (see 304 above).

Eucharistic Fast

110. Before receiving Holy Communion, the person should abstain from food and drink from at least one hour (Canon 919, paragraph 1).

110.1. If a person breaks that fast, he does not commit a sin.

110.2. Taking water or medicine is permitted and does not break the fast.

111. The sick or elderly and those who care for them may receive Holy Communion even if they have taken food or drink (Canon 919 paragraph 3).

Application: Missionaries should make not only doctors and nurses aware of this but families and friends as well. It is completely new.

112. Priests who celebrate a second or third Mass may take food and drink between these celebrations. He is only bound to observe the fast before the first Mass (Canon 919, paragraph 2).

Communion Twice a Day

113. Missionaries should instruct their people on this regulation, namely, that those who have already received Holy Communion may receive it *again and only if* they are participating in a Mass (Canon 917).

114. While, ordinarily, a priest should have at least one person attending Mass that he celebrates, it seems clear that, for a just and reasonable reason, a priest may celebrate completely alone.

Application: This legislation has changed. A just and reasonable reason could often occur in the mission lands where the priest has a village completely non-Catholic or his need to travel. One should not be too strict about this.

Consecration of the Bread and Wine

This regulation should probably be known by all priests.

115. It is absolutely forbidden, even in extreme cases, to consecrate the bread or wine without the other element or to consecrate them both outside the Eucharistic celebration (Canon 927).

Application: While this rule is probably known to all priests, there have been cases where missionaries have been distributing Holy Communion and run out of hosts, and then going to the sacristy and getting more hosts and consecrating them alone. It has happened, and I know of such cases.

Application: It has also happened that the priest, after the consecration, notices that water instead of wine was consecrated due to a mix-up in the cruets. In that case, he should remove the water and pour wine in the chalice and consecrate the wine. *Do not consecrate the bread again.*

Priests Recovering from Alcoholism

116. Priests recovering from alcoholism may receive communion by intinction. If they are concelebrating, they may receive communion only by the host.

117. Priests who cannot receive even a drop of wine may obtain from their ordinary permission to consecrate grape juice instead of wine.

117.1. According to authors, this grape juice should be *mustum.* Mustum is fresh grape juice or grape juice in which fermentation has been prevented by freezing or bottling.

Tridentine Mass

118. No permission is needed to celebrate the Tridentine Mass using the *Missale Romanum*, 1962 edition. Formerly, permission from the diocesan bishop was required, but now, this permission has been extended to all priests.

Time of Celebrating Mass

119. Mass can be celebrated any time of the day or night (Canon 931).

120. Anticipated evening Mass may be held only in the evening. It should not begin before 4:00 PM (Pius XII apostolic constitution, Christus Dominus).

Reservation of the Eucharist

121. A priest may not personally keep the Eucharist on himself or carry it with him unless there is pastoral necessity (Canon 935).

Application: The missionary may consecrate at one time and then bring the Eucharist with him as he goes to visit villages and give communion to the people and especially the sick. That is certainly within pastoral necessity.

Chapter Five

The Sacrament of Reconciliation

This is whereby the faithful, after confessing their sins and receiving absolution from a validly ordained priest, are reconciled with God and with the Church and with one another.

It is necessary to briefly review the theology of this sacrament in order to understand some of the applications that will be given.

The Nature of the Sacrament

> In the sacrament of penance the faithful who confess their sins to a legitimate minister, are sorry for them and intend to reform themselves obtain from God through the absolution imparted by the same minister forgiveness of the sins they have committed after Baptism. (Canon 959)

Individual Reconciliation

> Individual and integral confession and absolution constitute the only ordinary means by which a member of the faithful conscious of grave sin is reconciled with God and the Church. Only physical or moral impossibility excuses from confession of this type; in such a case reconciliation can be obtained by other means. (Canon 960)

These two canons summarize the general teaching of moral theology about confession. Methods and the law of general confession will be taken up in the following canons. There have been some radical teachings about confession that there is no need to confess mortal sins. The above two canons were printed just to remind the priests of the correct teaching of the Church.

Obligations for General Reconciliation

The rules for general confession are found in Canon 961, paragraphs 1 and 2. They are as follows:

> Absolution cannot be imparted in a general manner to many penitents at once without previous individual confessions unless;

1. Danger of death is imminent and there is insufficient time for the priest or priests to hear the confessions of the individual penitents;
2. There is a grave necessity, that is, when in view of the number of penitents, there are not enough confessors available to hear the confessions of the individuals properly within a suitable period of time in such a way that the penitents are forced to be deprived for a long while of sacramental grace or holy communion through no fault of their own. Sufficient necessity is not considered to exist when confessors cannot be present due only to a large number of penitents such as can occur on some great feast or pilgrimage. (Paragraph 1)

   It belongs to the diocesan bishop to judge whether the conditions required according to the norms of paragraph 1 and 2 are present. He can determine the cases of such necessity, attentive to the criteria agreed upon with the other members of the conference of bishops. (Paragraph 2)

Application: Paragraph 1 could easily take place in a mission land where the missionary cannot return to a large village for some time, and thus, the penitents would be deprived of Holy Communion for a long time. This would make an excellent topic for discussion in mission meetings. The *Commentary* has an excellent observation that may be helpful to missionaries.

> The extended deprivation of sacramental grace mentioned in the canon as a justifying general absolution refers to the grace of the sacrament of penance this deprivation may create a spiritual hardship for those not conscious of grave sin as well as for those conscious of grave sin and who would therefore be deprived not only of the sacramental penance, but also of sacramental communion.
>
> Finally the length of time is relatively understood, it could be several weeks or a month. It depends upon the locality and the missionary's travels etc. (Page 1147, paragraph 2)

The Minister of Reconciliation

As there have been certain changes and opinions dating from Vatican II, it is well to set out the proper rules of the faculties to hear confession.

> The priest alone is the minister for the sacrament of penance. (Canon 965)
>
> The valid absolution of sins requires that the minister have, in addition to the powers of orders, the faculty of exercising it for the faithful to whom he imparts absolution. (Canon 966, paragraph 1)

> A priest can be given the faculty either by the law itself or by a grant made by a competent authority according to the norms of Canon 969. (Canon 966, paragraph 2)

Application: By virtue of the law, pastors have the faculty to hear confessions within their own jurisdiction. However, the term *pastor* used in this canon refers to the strict meaning of *pastor*. In many mission territories, the term *parish* and *pastor* are used to facilitate matters. But they are not really *parishes* or *pastors* in the strict canonical sense. Parishes and quasi-parishes must be canonically erected, and pastors in the strict sense must be canonically appointed. Many missionaries are just assigned to a particular locality.

Missionary priests working on assignment in a particular diocese or vicariate will therefore require faculties from the bishop or prefect apostolic of the place (Canon 969, paragraph 1).

If the priest is a religious belonging to a clerical religious order, he should have the necessary faculties from his superiors as well.

Granting the Faculties

> Faculties can be given either for a definite or indefinite period of time. If the faculties are to be given for habitual use, they should be in writing. (Canon 972, 973)

> If a priest has faculties either by law or by delegation he can exercise them everywhere, unless a bishop has denied it in a particular place. (Canon 967, paragraph 2)

This is an extremely valuable faculty for missionary priests. Father X is a missionary in Z and has faculties there. He comes home to the USA on furlough and travels on fund-raising trips. He has faculties and does not have to ask for them.

Absolution in Danger of Death

Even though a priest lacks the faculties to hear confessions, he absolves licitly and validly any penitent whatsoever in danger of death from any censure or sins, even if an approved priest is present (Canon 976).

Application: This faculty is given by law and is extremely valuable for a missionary priest. Take for example even a priest in an inner-city mission situation who comes upon a person in danger of death. In danger of death does not mean the person is dying in extremis but simply is in a situation where he could be killed.

Revocation of Faculties

Canon 974 is very valuable in that it protects the priest from having his faculties revoked easily by the competent authority.

It reads, "The local ordinary and the competent authority are not to revoke the faculty to hear confessions habitually except for a grave cause" (Paragraph 1).

Ecclesia Supplet

In Ecclesia supplet, or the Church supplies, the faculty is important to know. I give the definition from *The Pastoral Companion* by Father John Huels, JD, on page 127:

> In common error of fact or law, the Church supplies executive power of governance for both external and internal forum. This norm also applies to the faculty for confession (Canon 144). The error concerns the existence of the faculty; it is based on the factual situation that gives rise to the belief that a priest has the faculty to hear confessions whereas in reality he does not.

Application: Father X is very new in the mission. He has studied the language. He goes to village Y. He thought he had faculties, but actually, he did not. He goes in the confessional, and the people line up and go to confession to him. This is a typical situation where the Church supplies the faculty because there was common error.

The Seal of Confession

While the missionary priest should already know what the Church teaches about the seal of the confessional, a brief summary is given in the handbook.

> The sacramental seal is inviolable. Therefore it is absolutely forbidden for the confessor to betray the penitent either by word, or any other means, for any reason. Also bound to the observance of secrecy is the interpreter, if there is one, and all others who have gained knowledge in any way of a sinner's confession. (Canon 983)

A direct violation of the seal is to reveal both the identity of the penitent and the sin.

An indirect violation of the seal occurs when, if from the things the confessor says or does, there raises the danger that others will come to know the sin confessed and the penitent.

A direct violation of the seal incurs an automatic excommunication reserved to the Apostolic See.

An indirect violation does not incur excommunication but can be punished according to the gravity of the situation (Canon 1388).

The confessor may discuss the sin with the penitent outside the confessional only if the penitent is willing to approach the confessor and discuss it with him.

Censures, Penalties, and Absolution

The subject of censures and absolution is too complicated for a handbook with the exception of three sins that incur automatic penalties and which the missionary priest may come across in his pastoral work. These are as follows:

- Procuring an abortion (Canon 1398). Automatic excommunication.

  Concerning abortion, the Commission for the Authentic Interpretation of the Code has declared that this is to be understood not only the ejection of the immature fetus, but also the killing of the fetus procuring in any manner and any time from the moment of conception. Excommunication means the person is prohibited from (1) having any ministerial participation of the Eucharist or any other ceremonies of worship, (2) celebrating the sacraments or sacramentals and receiving the sacraments, (3) exercising any ecclesiastical offices, ministries, functions, or placing acts of governance (Canon 1331, paragraph 1).

- Attempting marriage, even civilly, by a lay religious in perpetual vows. Automatic interdict.

  Automatic interdict means the brother or sister is prohibited from any ministerial participation in the celebration of the Eucharist or any other ceremonies of worship and celebrating the sacraments or sacramentals and receiving the sacraments.

- A cleric who attempts marriage, even civil, incurs automatic suspension (Canon 1384, paragraph 1).

  Suspension prohibits the celebration of the sacraments and sacramentals or placing any act of governance.

Since the sin of abortion is the one incurring a penalty and is the one most commonly met by a missionary priest in his pastoral work, this can be found not only among the uneducated faithful but also doctors, nurses, midwives, and health-care personnel. Hence, the priest should keep in mind those exempt from any penalties:

- Anyone under the age of sixteen
- Anyone inculpable ignorant of the law
- One who violates the law out of grave fear, if only relatively grave

- One lacking the use of reason

In the sin of abortion, it is good to ask these questions, and if the answer is *yes*, then the censure is not incurred:

- Was it only an attempted abortion that did not succeed, or was it only indirect such as a hysterectomy to remove a deceased uterus?
- Was the penitent ignorant, through no fault of his or her own, that a penalty was attached to the act?
- Was the abortion accidental or not intentional?
- Did the penitent have the imperfect use of reason, e.g., mental retardation, psychologically disturbed, etc.?
- Did the penitent act out of fear, e.g., parental fear, criminal offense, prison, etc.?

The above, taken from *The Pastoral Companion*, page 145ff, may be of a help to determine if a penitential crime was committed.

Remission of the Censure

The following have the power to remit the censure of excommunication of the sin of abortion:

- All ordinaries (Canon 1355, paragraph 2)

- All bishops in the confessional (Canon 1355, paragraph 2)
- All priests who are chaplains in hospitals, prisons, and on sea voyages (Canon 566, paragraph 2)
- Any confessor in the internal forum if remaining in the state of sin for the time necessary to receive a remission from the Apostolic See would be hard on the penitent (Canon 1357, paragraph 2)

However, this refers only to automatic excommunication and interdicts and not, I repeat, not to suspension.

Application: Father X is hearing confessions. A priest Father Y comes to him and is clearly upset. He is known to Father X. Y is sobbing and confesses what Father X already knows. Y had left the priesthood, got married with a local girl by a judge. And what is worse, he had her obtain an abortion as he did not want children. Between sobs, he begs forgiveness and is truly sorry for his sins. Father X calms him down, tells him he will be back shortly, goes to the rectory, and pulls out his handbook and reads up on abortion, then goes back. Father X tells Y he can remove the censure of excommunication from the abortion, but he cannot remove the suspension. That will have to go to the Apostolic See. He gives Y an appropriate penance, absolves him of his sins, and tells him the suspension matter he will have to handle the matter without mentioning any name (Canon 1357, paragraph 1, 2).

Every diocese should have developed policies to assist the confessors in handling such cases.

When Father X absolves Y of his sins, he has the intention of also remitting the censure, and therefore, no special formula is needed, just the usual one, "I absolve you," etc.

In Danger of Death

Any priest, even if he does not have faculties to hear confessions, can validly absolve a penitent from any censure, and he can do so even if a priest is present who has faculties to remit censures (Canon 976).

The canon says, "Danger of death." This does not mean he is sick or dying, but just in danger of dying; it could be from being killed, executed, etc.

Chapter Six

The Sacrament of Holy Orders

This is whereby the faithful are provided with bishops, priests, and deacons to fulfill the sacred function of the sacraments and to provide guidance and teaching in the true faith and magisterium of the Church.

This handbook will not provide information on the matter and form of the sacrament but, instead, will indicate only a few rights and obligations of priests, referring to their missionary life and labors.

The following are the strongest obligations:

1. Obedience: A special obligation binds priests to reverence and obedience to the Supreme Pontiff and his ordinary (Canon 273).
2. Fidelity to duties: Unless there is a legitimate impediment excusing them, priests are bound to undertake and

faithfully fulfill the duty entrusted to them by their ordinary (Canon 274, paragraph 2).

3. Holiness: Priests are especially bound to pursue holiness in living their lives since they are consecrated to God in orders by a new title as stewards of the mysteries of God in the service of his people (Canon 276, paragraph 1).
4. Divine Office: Priests are bound by obligation to recite the Liturgy of the Hours (Canon 276, paragraph 2, 3).
5. Retreat: Priests are required to make a retreat as prescribed by the local law.
6. Celibacy: Priests are bound by obligation to observe perfect and perpetual continence for the sake of the kingdom of heaven and, therefore, to observe celibacy, which is a special gift from God by which sacred ministers can remain close to Christ with an undivided heart and can more freely dedicate themselves to the service of God and humanity. (Canon 277, paragraph 1).

The above are provided for the missionary priest's own reflection and meditation and are not referred to any faculties.

Chapter Seven

The Sacrament of Matrimony

This is whereby a man and woman confer on themselves the sacrament of marriage through the matrimonial consent, which is an act of the will in which each party mutually gives and accepts each other through an irrevocable covenant in order to establish marriage and which is witnessed by a minister of the Church.

101. When two unbaptized persons marry, the Church claims no jurisdiction; therefore, there are no faculties pertaining to this marriage.

102. Marriage between a Catholic and baptized non-Catholic are subject to both divine and canon law as well as the competence of the civil law.

102.1. To be a sacramental marriage, both parties must be baptized whether by a Catholic baptism or a valid non-Catholic baptism.

102.2. All marriages, even between two non-Catholics, must be free of divine impediments that are not contrary to the divine law of indissolubility—the necessity of giving true consent to marriage—and free from such impediments as impotence.

Faculty to Witness a Marriage

103. If the missionary priest is pastor in the strict canonical meaning of a parish, he may, by virtue of the law, validly assist at a marriage of his own subjects and of those nonsubjects within the parish boundaries.

103.1. If the missionary priest is pastor in the canonical sense, he may delegate the faculty to validly assist at a marriage to a priest or deacon (Canon 137, paragraph 3).

103.2. If the missionary is pastor in the noncanonical sense, then he needs faculties from the ordinary to validly assist at marriages. Hence, associate pastors also require the faculty from the ordinary.

Dispensation from the Form of Marriage

104. Dispensation from the form of marriage means that the marriage may take place without the witness of a priest or deacon.

104.1. The requirement for this dispensation must be the presence of a serious difficulty.

104.2. For validity, there must be some form of public action that expresses the mutual will of the two parties to enter marriage.

Application: Some missionary priests will be in the situation where they can go to a village only once or twice a year. In the priest's absence, the local people hold their customary ceremonies of marriage. When the priest arrives, he should recognize these marriages as valid unions and conduct only some blessing rather then "remarrying" the couple.

Common-Law Marriages

105. A common-law marriage is one in which the couple express true matrimonial consent but without any public celebration or form. It is not the same as "just living together."

105.1. If the common-law marriages are valid in the civil law, they are also valid for marriages between Protestants and the unbaptized.

105.2. Common-law marriages are *not* valid for Catholics, either when both parties are Catholic or when only one party is Catholic. To be valid, they must have some sort of public celebration as indicated above in 104.

Impediments to Marriage

106. The impediment of age. Marriage of a male who has not completed his sixteenth year and of a female who has not completed her fourteenth year is invalid.

106.1. Except in case of necessity, the priest is not to assist at the marriage of a minor, i.e., anyone under the age of eighteen whose parents are unaware of the marriage or reasonably opposed to it (Canon 1071, paragraph 1, 6).

Application: The customary law in mission lands differs considerably. In some localities, children are marked for marriage at a very young age. Some, especially the girls, are forced into marriage at a very early age.

107. The impediment of impotence.

108. The impediment of prior bond.

108.1. This impediment binds both Catholic and non-Catholic. The prior bond must be declared invalid by a competent authority before a Catholic can enter a marriage or by a dissolution of the prior bond by a competent authority.

108.2. If the prior bond was a *lack of form case*—that is, a Catholic contracted marriage, for example, by a civil authority—a declaration of invalidity by a competent authority is not required. However, Canon 1071, paragraph 1 to 3 requires the permission of the ordinary when the party has natural obligations such as children. This can be delegated, and the missionary priest should be aware of this.

109. The impediment of disparity of cult. This impediment comes when a baptized Catholic marries a person who is not baptized.

Application: The missionary priest will frequently come upon cases where a Catholic has already married civilly an unbaptized person or the situation will arise in the premarriage investigation. The power to dispense from this impediment differs from diocese or diocese. Hence, the missionary should make certain that he has the faculty to dispense or, if not, then is able to petition the ordinary for the dispensation.

110. The impediment of holy orders.

111. The impediment of perpetual vows of a religious.

Application: It is quite possible that the missionary comes across a religious who has left the institute without a dispensation from his or her religious vows. In danger of death, a confessor can dispense this impediment.

112. The impediment of abduction.

113. The impediment of crime arises when either one or both parties commit murder of the other person's spouse in order to contract marriage.

114. The impediment of consanguinity. In the direct line, this impediment arises with all ancestors and descendants; that is, grandfather, grandmother, mother, son, grandson, granddaughter. In the collateral line, it invalidates to the fourth degree, i.e., brother-sister (second degree), aunt-nephew, uncle-niece (third degree), first cousins, or great aunts, great nephews (fourth degree).

Application: A dispensation from the direct line or the second-degree collateral line is never given. The local ordinary can dispense from the third and fourth collateral line. However, and this is very important if such cases arise, the missionary must know the civil law of the place or the customary law and never seek a dispensation when these laws are invalidating a marriage.

115. The impediment of affinity. This impediment arises from the husband and the blood relation of the wife or of the wife and the blood relations of the husband.

Application: The customary or civil law has an application here, and the missionary should be aware of this. Likewise, in some places, the civil impediment ceases upon the death of a spouse.

116. The impediment of public propriety. This impediment arises in concubinage and between the man and his lover's blood relations or the woman and her lover's blood relations. For example, a man X is living with a concubine Y who has a daughter from a previous relationship. X wants to marry the daughter.

117. The impediment of legal relationship. This impediment arises from a civil adoption.

118. The impediment of spiritual relationship arises between the baptized and the godparents.

Convalidation Because of an Impediment

119. There are no faculties to convalidate a marriage because of an impediment. However, there may be a convalidation such as automatically, e.g., prior bond but the previous spouse dies or ages.

119.1. A renewal of consent is not required since the consent given initially, and has not been revoked, is still valid.

119.2. However, the diocese may have regulations regarding the convalidation of an impediment since the matter can be complicated. Hence, the missionary should be familiar with the diocesan policy.

Convalidation of Defective Consent

120. Because of the complexities in this convalidation, it is best that the diocese also has a policy as to how this should be handled.

Convalidation of Defective Form

121. There are two types of defective form: (1) when the parties contract marriage completely outside the Catholic Church as, for example, in front of a civil authority such as a judge, or (2)

the marriage lacked a substantial form due to the absence of an essential element, such as the lack of the faculty to assist at marriage by the minister or before only one witness.

121.1. Convalidation can take place with a renewal of consent according to the canonical sense, i.e., before a minister with faculties and two witnesses (Canon 1160).

Application: The missionary will come across defective-form cases rather often in his pastoral work. Again, the diocese should have a policy as to how these cases are handled since there may also be a diriment impediment or a need for a dispensation.

Premarriage Instructions

There are no faculties to the priest regarding the premarriage instructions. The diocese should have the proper policy regarding this.

Dissolution of the Bond

In many dioceses, the dissolution of the bond will involve the bishop and a canon lawyer. However, the missionary priest must be able to recognize the possibility of such cases and will be involved in the practical handling of the cases.

The dissolution of the bond is not a case of annulment. They are cases in which a bond of marriage is actually existing but is dissolved.

The two main avenues in which this can come about are the Pauline Privilege and the Petrine Privilege.

122. The Pauline Privilege is based on 1 Corinthians 7:12-15.

> If any brother has a wife who is not a believer, and she is willing to go on living with him, he should not divorce her; and if any wife has a husband who is an unbeliever, and he is willing to go on living with her, she should not divorce her husbands. For the unbelieving husband is made holy through his wife, and the unbelieving wife is made holy through the brother. Otherwise your children would be unclean, whereas in fact they are clean.
>
> If the unbeliever separates, let him separate. The brother or sister is not bound in such cases. God has called you to peace.

123. In short, this means that the marriage of two unbaptized persons can be dissolved in favor of the faith of the one who becomes baptized provided that the unbaptized party departs.

Application: The missionary will frequently come across such cases as this one. X the husband and Y his wife were married according to custom in the village. Both were non-Christians. After some years, Y leaves X and becomes a second wife to M. X finds a new wife H, also unbaptized. Now X wants to become a Catholic. In the prenuptial inquiry, the missionary discovers that X was previously married to Y, who ran away from him. There are grounds here for a Pauline Privilege.

The Interpellations

124. The interpellations or questions must be put to Y, the wife who ran away from X. They are the following:

1. Do you, Y, also want to become a Catholic and be baptized? and
2. Are you willing to cohabit peacefully with X, who is becoming a Catholic?

124.1. The unbaptized party, Y, must be given sufficient time to answer these questions. If after a period of time Y does not answer, then a negative answer can be taken for granted.

125. The local ordinary can dispense from the interpellations altogether. If X and Y were actually divorced either through a civil court or by custom, this is sufficient reason to omit the interpellations.

126. In the case where the new wife H does not want to become a Catholic but wants to remain unbaptized, the case can proceed as one of mixed marriage.

The Petrine Privilege

127. The Petrine Privilege means that a marriage entered by parties, at least one of whom is not baptized, can be dissolved by the Roman pontiff in favor of the faith as long as the marriage was not consummated after both parties received baptism.

Application: What generally happens is this example. X and Y are both unbaptized, and both want to become Catholics. In the catechumenate, it is found out that X, the husband, was married by custom years ago to M, also unbaptized. But the marriage did not last, and M left X and was married to another man. Father sees here that there is a case where the marriage of X and M can be dissolved by the Holy Father. This is a typical case of the Petrine Privilege.

127.1. The Congregation of the Doctrine of Faith is competent to handle the case in Rome. Hence, the local ordinary is the one who will instruct that the case be drafted and sent to that congregation.

127.2. To receive the dissolution, two things are required, and these are what are investigated on the local level:

1. There is no possibility of restoring the marriage between X and M, and
2. The petitioner, in this case X, was not at least exclusively the cause of the breakdown of the marriage with M.

128. Another typical case of the Petrine Privilege is when X is already a Catholic and he wants to marry Z, who is unbaptized but was married to C, also unbaptized. Z has no intention to become a Catholic, but X and Z want their marriage approved by the Church. The same procedure is followed, in this case with an exception. Z must agree—and in writing, if this is possible, signed by X and Z—that Z will allow X to practice his religion and any children will be raised as Catholics.

Application: As the above two cases can frequently arise in the mission lands, the missionary priest should be aware of them. Likewise, the mission diocese should have a suitable catechumenate and prenuptial questionnaire, which, if followed, will expose such cases.

Polygamous Marriages

Former faculties granted to missionaries, these were Constitutions Altitudo, granted by Pope Paul III, June 1, 1537; Constitution Romani Pontificis, Pius VI, August 2, 1571; and Constitution Populis, Gregory XIII, January 25, 1585. All these faculties are now found in Canons 1148 and 1149.

129. "A non baptized man who simultaneously has several unbaptized wives can keep one of them and dismiss the others if he finds it difficult to live with the first wife. The same is applicable to a woman who had several simultaneous husbands" (Canon 1148).

129.1. The local ordinary should bear in mind the social needs of the dismissed wives or husbands and that these are met.

130. "An unbaptized person who after baptism is unable to restore cohabitation with his s or her spouse because of captivity or persecution, may contract a new marriage even if the former spouse was baptized" (Canon 1149).

Application: There could be a possibility of using this canon if e.g., the husband was sentenced to life or a long prison term. According to the *Commentary*, this dissolution takes place by the law; hence, it does not have to go to Rome. It would be wise, however, to take the case to the local ordinary so that a diocesan policy can be observed if there is one.

The Internal Forum Solution

131. The internal forum solution to convalidate marriages is *not* a canonical solution and is generally not found in canon law works. It is given in this handbook because it is a solution used by

some priests especially when it is found that there are difficulties in determining the invalidity of a previous marriage.

The internal forum solution is a theory used by some that a person has been married, then divorced and the first marriage is considered invalid but the invalidity cannot be proven in the ecclesiastical tribunal. This opinion considers that the remarried Catholic should not be deprived of the sacraments of reconciliation and the Eucharist because they are unable to prove the invalidity of the previous marriage.

There are various reasons why the invalidity of the first marriage cannot be proven, such as the lack of witnesses to provide grounds on the invalidity or the impossibility of the first spouse to be found and give testimony, or there may be medical grounds but these cannot be proven because of a lack of records.

In the internal forum, the Catholic party can receive the sacraments as long as there is no scandal given to the faithful community such as by receiving the sacraments in another parish.

The condition laid down in using the internal forum is that the Catholic party will promise to have the present marriage validated if the previous spouse died.

The following must be noted:

1. The priest does *not* convalidate the marriage of the person seeking a solution to his or her married problem.
2. The priest must *not* perform any sort of marriage ceremony for the person.

The person must be able to understand that their present irregular marriage is still irregular as far as the Church is concerned.

The internal forum solution is, generally speaking, not a solution that can be performed within the short time of a confession. The priest must make certain that the person seeking this solution is able to understand what it is.

Application: Many missionary priests may find that the use of the internal forum is very difficult to apply in the mission-land context. In providing this above information, the author neither recommends nor disapproves the internal forum solution but provides this solution as pastoral information used by some. It is entirely up to the missionary priest whether he uses this solution or not.

For further information, note *internal forum solution* on the Web site, also *A Theology of Christian Marriage* by Michael Lawler, the Liturgical Press.

Chapter Eight

The Sacrament of the Anointing of the Sick

This is whereby the faithful who are seriously ill are anointed with the sacred oil by a priest and receive the grace of the Holy Spirit to assist them in their sickness with spiritual fortitude.

101. The anointing of the sick can be traced back to apostolic times. It was alluded to by Mark 6:13 and clearly spoken of by St. James in chapter 5:14-15. Over the course of time, the practice of imparting the sacrament became more and more given when a person was close to death; hence, it was frequently called extreme unction or the last rites. The Second Vatican Council, however, in the apostolic constitution Sacram Unctionem Infirmorum, directed that the sacrament of the anointing of the sick be given to those who are seriously ill by anointing them with blessed oil on the forehead and hands.

The Matter and Form

102. The matter of the sacrament is blessed oil, either olive oil or oil from a plant that has been blessed as oil for the sick.

102.1. The oil for the sick is usually blessed by a bishop on Holy Thursday. The priest who keeps the oil, such as chaplains and pastors, should make certain that they use oil that was blessed at the last Mass of the Chrism. Oil that is old should not be used unless of necessity but should be absorbed on cotton or cloth and burned.

102.2. Generally speaking, the blessing of the oil for the anointing of the sick is performed by a bishop or anyone equated in law to a diocesan bishop. However, in case of necessity, any priest may bless the oil provided he does so during the celebration of the sacrament (Canon 999).

102.3. While the blessed oil should be kept in a reasonably decent place and the priest may carry with him the sacred oil for one never knows when he may come across a seriously sick person, priests do not need any special faculty or permission to carry with them the sacred oil or to anoint a seriously sick person.

103. The form of the anointing is as follows:

"Through this holy anointing, may the Lord in His love and mercy help you with the grace of the Holy Spirit. May He who frees you from sin save you and raise you up."

103.1. The first part of the form is recited while the priest anoints the person on the forehead. The second part is said while he anoints the hands.

103.2. The entire formula is required for validity, but the division of anointing on the forehead and hands is recommended but does not affect validity.

103.3. The anointing of the hand is on the palms except when anointing a priest; the anointing may be on the back of the hands.

103.4. If there is a necessity as, for example, a risk of contagion, the anointing may be done by using an instrument such as a stick or forceps with cotton attached.

104. The minister of the sacrament.

The sacrament of the anointing of the sick may be performed only by a validly ordained priest. Deacons do not have the capacity by virtue of their ordination to the diaconate.

104.1. No special faculty is required to administer this sacrament.

105. The recipient of the sacrament.

To validly receive the sacrament of the anointing of the sick, a person must have the use of reason and begin to fall into danger of death because of sickness or old age.

105.1. Children may be anointed if they have reached the age of reason.

105.2. A person who obstinately does not want to receive the sacrament should not be anointed because they lack the proper intention to receive the sacrament.

105.3. The person must be in serious danger healthwise to be anointed. A soldier about to go into battle or a criminal to be executed cannot be given the sacrament because the sacrament can only be given to those seriously sick.

105.4. A person to undergo surgery may be anointed if the surgery is due to a serious illness. The person does not have to be dying but rather seriously ill. Likewise, it is not necessary that the person be awake or knows what is happening as, for example, if the person is in a coma, the anointing may take place.

105.5. The anointing of a person in old age may be performed if the person is weak. While one should not be too scrupulous regarding this, if old people ask for the sacrament, it should be given them as sometimes an elderly person may sense his or her own weakened state.

105.6. While not every coming to the attention of a priest may be one where he cannot administer the sacrament, for example, an ordinary sick person but not seriously sick or even a non-Christian who is sick and asks or a priest (or deacon) to bless him or her, the Church has liturgical blessings for the sick and persons otherwise, such as prisoners or soldiers. It is advised that priests or deacons in an active ministry have handy a small booklet with such blessings.

105.7. If there is a doubt as to whether the person is seriously ill or properly disposed or even if the person is dead, the anointing of the sick may take place.

105.8. If the person is definitely dead, the priest should not administer the sacrament even conditionally. If the person's heart has ceased to beat, the process of dying is not immediate but takes places over some time, perhaps even to an hour. But when the person is definitely dead, the priest should recite the prayers for the dead.

106. Any of the faithful who are seriously sick can and should be given viaticum, that is, Holy Communion. Children who have not yet reached the use of reason may, however, receive viaticum provided they are able to distinguish the body of Christ from ordinary food.

Chapter Nine

Special Blessings and Circumstances

This is in which the missionary priest may be called upon to give the blessing of the Church to objects, persons, and places.

101. Sacramentals are sacred signs by which, similar to sacraments, particular spiritual effects are signified and obtained by the intercession of the Church (Canon 1166).

102. Only the Apostolic See can establish new sacramentals, interpret authentically those already accepted, or abolish or change them. In confecting or administering the sacramentals, the rites and formulas approved by the authority of the Church are to be observed (Canon 1167).

102.1. Sacramentals may be actions or materials things.

102.2. The sacramental actions are official rites of the Church, such as consecrations, dedications, blessings, exorcisms, funeral rites, religious profession, institutions, the coronation of images of the Blessed Virgin, and commission of various ministries. These sacramentals are transitory.

102.3. Other sacramentals are things that are used over and over, such as holy oil, holy water, blessed ashes, blessed palms, blessed metals, and blessed scapulars.

The Ministers of Sacramentals

103. The minister of sacramentals is a cleric who has the power either by law or delegation.

103.1. To a lesser extent, a lay person may assist in administering a sacramental, such as in distributing ashes on Ash Wednesday.

Consecrations and Dedications

104. A consecration or dedication means that the place, person, or object is set aside for divine worship or for the service of the Church.

104.1. The dedication of a church pertains to the diocesan bishop, which can be delegated to another bishop or in urgent cases to a priest (Canon 1206).

104.2. The consecration of virgins should be done by the diocesan bishop or delegated to another bishop or even a priest in urgent cases.

104.3. The bishop or major superiors may delegate a priest to preside at the institution of lectors and acolytes.

104.4. The consecration of sacred chrism is reserved for validity to a bishop.

Ministers of Blessings

105. The ordinary ministers of blessings are bishops and priests. The blessings may be given to persons, places, or things.

105.1. Generally, the priest will bless objects such as a metal, rosary, or an animal by a simple sign of the cross over the object. He may also sprinkle holy water on the blessed object.

Application: Many missionary priests will be working where they have many villages to visit. In some cases, there will be a central mission station that has a church. This church, which has the reservation of the Blessed Sacrament, should be blessed by the bishop if possible. The villages may possibly have a small dwelling where the village people gather together for prayer or for Sunday devotions conducted by a prayer leader or catechist. The small village chapel can be blessed by the missionary as a sign they are dedicated for worship and not used for other purposes.

105.2. To erect the stations of the cross, the missionary will need the faculty from the local ordinary, or if there is a Franciscan friar on hand, he can do so. The rite is simply making the way of the cross, which entails a brief meditation on each station.

105.3. To gain the indulgence, the station must have a cross of either wood or plastic. Painting the cross on the wall is not sufficient.

Exorcisms

Missionaries who are working in a very non-Christian area will probably come upon cases of demoniac possession. He should keep the following in mind:

106. No one may lawfully perform exorcisms unless he has obtained the special and expressed permission of the local ordinary. This permission is to be granted by the local ordinary only to a priest endowed with piety, wisdom, prudence, and integrity of life (Canon 1172).

106.1. It is evident from this canon that the Church wants the priest who will perform exorcism to be well prepared and that he be a priest known for his holiness and purity of life.

Otherwise, cases in the past have shown that the devil attacks the priest even physically and exposes his own shortcomings.

106.2. This canon does not forbid the exorcism in the catechumenate or infant baptism nor in simple prayers used to bless a person. It refers to cases where there is actual evidence of devil possession.

106.3. Persons with certain psychological disorders should not be taken for cases of possessions. Hence, the missionary should be aware of such mental illnesses and take counsel with others, especially more experienced priests.

106.4. For those who wish to have further information, there is considerable information on the Internet on demoniac possession and the Church.

Funeral Rites for the Dead

107. Prohibited days for funerals. While funeral masses may be celebrated on any day, they should not be celebrated on holy days of obligation, Holy Thursday, the Easter triduum, and the Sundays of Advent, Lent, and of the Easter season.

Application: While this is the general rule, it may well happen in a mission land that it is necessary to bury the people quickly. Common sense should prevail.

Cremation

108. Cremation is not forbidden unless it is being carried out for reasons contrary to Christian belief, such as denial of the resurrection (Canon 1176, paragraph 3).

Catholics Who Are Denied Catholic Funeral Rites

109. Unless before death there was some sign of repentance, ecclesiastical funeral rites are denied to notorious apostates, heretics, and schismatic for reasons, those who have chosen cremation for reasons contrary to the Christian faith, and other manifest sinners for whom ecclesiastical funeral rites cannot be conducted without public scandal to the faithful (Canon 1184, paragraph 1).

Application: The decision in such cases may require considerable weighing of the reasons and even consultation with the bishop.

Liturgies of Marriage

Marriage between a Catholic and Another Christian

110. Members of other churches may be witnesses at the celebration of marriage in a Catholic Church. Likewise, Catholics may be witnesses of a marriage celebrated in another church (Cong Doct Faith, 136).

111. A Catholic priest may assist in some way in a non-Catholic Christian church with the permission of the ordinary when the marriage is a mixed marriage and there has been a dispensation from the form of marriage.

112. The local ordinary may permit the priest, at the request of the marrying parties, to invite a minister of another church to participate in the wedding ceremonies; but the priest is the one who receives the marriage vows. The minister may give an exhortation or blessing.

112.1. Regarding the sharing of the Eucharist in a mixed marriage, see the above section on non-Catholic sharing of the Eucharist above.

Index

A

abduction. *See* marriage: impediments to
abortion, 54-56
absolution, 46-47, 49, 51, 54
adult, 23
affinity. *See* marriage: impediments to
age. *See* marriage: impediments to
alcoholism, priests recovering from, 43
anointing of the sick, sacrament of the, 77-81
Apostolic See, 53, 57, 82

B

baptism
  of blood. *See* baptism: of desire
  of children, 21-23
  conditional, 26-27
  danger of death, 18-19
  of desire, 19
  Eucharist and, 28-29
  form and matter of, 24-25, 26
  minister for, 18
  in non-Catholic churches, 26
blessings, 82-84
bond
  dissolution of, 69-70
  prior. *See* marriage: impediments to

C

catechumen, 19-20
catechumenate, 19-21, 86
censures, 54, 56, 56-58
chrism, 29-30, 33, 78, 84
confessor, 53-54, 66

confirmation, sacrament of, 28-31, 34
Congregation for the Evangelization of Peoples, 14
consanguinity. *See* marriage: impediments to
consecration, 83-84
of bread and wine, 42-44
of sacred chrism, 84
convalidation, 68-69
cremation, 87
crime. *See* marriage: impediments to

D

dedication, 83
disparity of cult. *See* marriage: impediments to
Divine Word Missionaries, 13

E

Ecclesia Supplet, 52
Eucharist
to children. *See* Holy Communion: to children
in mixed marriage, 88
prohibition. *See* Holy Communion: prohibition
reservation of, 44-45
rights to, 37
sacrament of, 35
exorcism, 82, 85-86

F

faculties
to convalidate marriage, 68
former, 73
granting of, 33, 50-51
to preach, 36
revocation of, 51-52
to witness marriage, 62
faith, in favor of, 2, 20
funeral rites, 86-87

G

grape juice, 43-44

H

Holy Communion
to children, 40
ministers for, 36
prohibition, 39
reception of by baptized non-Catholic, 38
of the sick. *See* viaticum
holy orders, sacrament of, 59-60

homily, 37
Huels, Fr. John, 52
  Pastoral Companion, The, 52, 56

I

impediments. *See* marriage: impediments to
impotence. *See* marriage: impediments to
infant, 24, 86
internal forum solution, 74-76
interpellations, 71

L

Lawler, Michael, 76
  Theology of Christian Marriage, A, 76

M

marriage
  catechumenate and, 20
  common-law, 63-64
  dispensation from form of, 63
  faculty to witness, 62
  impediments to, 23-24, 28, 30, 55-56, 62, 64-67, 68, 80
  liturgies of, 87
  mixed, 72, 88
  polygamous, 73-74
Mass
  of the Chrism, 78
  preaching at, 36
minor, 24
mustum. *See* grape juice

N

Nihil Obstat, 21

P

Pastoral Companion, The (Huels), 52, 56
Pauline Privilege, 71
perpetual vows. *See* marriage: impediments to
Petrine Privilege, 72, 73
premarriage instructions, 69

R

reconciliation, sacrament of, 46-47, 49

S

sacramentals, 54-55, 82-83
Sacram Unctionem Infirmorum, 77

Sacred Congregation of the Propagation of the Faith. *See* Congregation for the Evangelization of Peoples
seal of the confessional, 54
Second Vatican Council, 77
stations of the cross, 85

T

Theology of Christian Marriage, A (Lawler), 76

V

viaticum, 40, 81

www.ingramcontent.com/pod-product-compliance
Ingram Content Group UK Ltd.
Pitfield, Milton Keynes, MK11 3LW, UK
UKHW041926190726
13854UKWH00003B/1464